BEGINNINGS

"A SMILE AND LAUGHTER ARE OLDER THAN SORROW.
THAT IS WHAT THE OLD ONES USED TO SAY."

Bertha Dan [Qual-so-litza], Swinomish

Beginnings

A Meditation on Coast Salish Lifeways

By Patrick J. Twohy

Library of Congress Catalog Card Number: 00 090706
ISBN: 0-9623418-1-9

First Edition, 1999
Second Edition, 2003

Publisher: Patrick J. Twohy

Design: Ann Amberg

This edition of *Beginnings* is made possible by funds from the Lummi,
Swinomish, and Tulalip Tribes, Neil and Marya Moses of Tulalip,
Bob and Diann Mize, and Jesuits of the Oregon Province.

Any money from retail sales of this book and all donations will be
used to cover further printing expenses and to fund the Swinomish
Intertribal Youth Programs.

Any questions regarding the book may be addressed to:

Swinomish Spiritual Center at St. Pauls Mission
Box 2100
La Conner, WA 98257
Fax: 360-466-4039

Prepress and printing by Rainier Color, Seattle, Washington, USA

To the Grandmothers and the Grandfathers

For Ella Acquino, Myrtle Bailey, Velma Cayou, Philomena Cheer,
Laura Edwards, Rose Fryberg, Gwen Hatch, Violet Hillaire,
Linette McKay, Theresa Moses, Betty Sampson, Jackie Tom,
Laura Wilbur, Pauline Twohy

For Bobby Bailey, Herbie Bill, Sam Cagey, Clarence Cheer,
Lawrence Edwards, Jr., Tim Edwards, Cyrus James, Jr.,
Landy James, Art Lane, Kenny Moses, Sr., Isadore Tom,
George Twohy, George Williams

All my Teachers

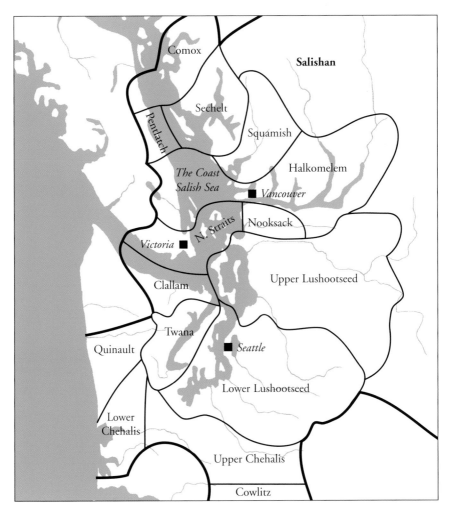

MAP OF COAST SALISH COUNTRY WITH LINGUISTIC AREAS NOTED

Part One

The Ancient and the Holy

THE NEW BEINGS

*"It is not what is happening today
that is as important as our history.
We have to know our history to keep
our identity as a People alive."*

BERTHA DAN [QUAL-SO-LITZA], SWINOMISH

*"When I was young I went to visit those
living up in the mountains. The grandmothers
used to pat me on the head and tell me to listen
because they would be going away. I didn't
understand what they meant. Where were they going?
Now I understand and feel bad that I didn't listen."*

RAYMOND MOSES [TI-AT-MUS], SNOHOMISH

Let us begin with the memories of the great-grandmothers,
The grandmothers and the grandfathers,
With all that they were told and all that they have seen,
Memories that stretch back to the terror and wonder
Of seeing the new beings who appeared one day
In the wide bays where the ancient rivers
Ran their way to the sea.

The People thought that they were spirits
Riding high over the water in large canoes
That moved through the mist like islands with trees.
Sounds traveled over the waters, strange to the ear.

There was an older memory among the People
That these beings had come once before.
The old ones remembered stories of hats that reflected
Light like the moon at quarter, hats with plumes
Stiff and unyielding. There was the memory
Of a strange sickness that scarred the People's faces,
And of something like the stumps of trees, with mouths
That threw out flames and smoke, hurling rocks
That tore holes in the air, the water, the earth,
In any living thing.

The men went out to the new beings.
Riding in wide cedar canoes, they went out
With songs that gave them strength,
Songs that would tell the new beings who they were.
These new beings looked like bears;

Their bodies seemed to be covered with hair.
The smell coming from their tall canoes
Was not pleasant. Their smaller canoes crawled
On the water like giant spiders.

These beings would shout and hold up hides
Of animals that the People knew well, sea otter,
Fur seal, beaver, pointing to the furs shining
And then to large clubs with edges sharp as chipped flint.

They lifted up blankets, woven tight, longer
And wider than the People's goat and dog hair capes.
They held out what looked like stone baskets
And round beads and buttons that even in the mist
Seemed to hold the color of the sky.

BEFORE THE NEW BEINGS CAME

"My granddaughter asked me, 'What is unique about Indian culture?' I told her, 'Our culture is the only one from here. The others are from other places.'"

ROBERT JOE, SR. [WA-WAL-TON], SWINOMISH

"The People considered the cedar tree as a great gift from the Creator. The cedar bends before it breaks. It would be good if we all could learn to bend before we break."

KENNY MOSES, SR. [KHWA-KHWAY-CHUB], SNOQUALMIE

Before these new beings came,
The People lived all along the rivers
And on the best beaches of the wide bays
That faced out to the neighboring islands guarding
Pathways to the deeper waters of the sea.
The People were gentle and generous
To visiting family and friends.
Large families lived in long homes

Framed with cedar posts and beams, roofed and walled
With cedar planks split with elk horn and yew wood wedges
From the north side of the tall trees that joined
The powers of sky and earth for as far
As even the eagle could see.

Cedar, strong and lasting;
Cedar roots stripped for the fibers to weave baskets,
Round, tight, beautiful to the eye,
Capable of holding berries or boiling water;
Baskets lasting for generations,
The gift of grandmother to granddaughter;

Cedar logs, pliable when steamed with heated
Rocks for the width of family canoes,
Agile and light upon the waters;
Cedar strands, pounded and woven,
Soft and warm to protect head and body
During the long winter rains;

Cedar posts guarding the doorways
And corners of the long family homes;
Cedar wood for carving bowls in animal forms;
Cedar poles and masks for the winter ceremonies;
Cedar strands for headgear and capes woven
Together with the white hair of mountain goats;
Cedar boughs for renewing a dancer's legs
Cold from swimming in the high mountain streams;
Cedar for removing a hunter's scent,
Or for brushing off the weight of sadness.

The Gifts of Food

"I have seen sixty pound salmon high up in the mountains. The meat was red with a brown layer of fat that was his food and energy for such a long journey."

Marya Moses, Snohomish

"The Long House used to be loaded with strings of horse clams. They were a delicacy for us. Sometimes we had nothing else to eat. We used to help our grandmothers wash them."

Laura Edwards [Ta-leq-tale], Lummi-Lower Skagit

On the beaches and under the waters of the bays
Held in the arms of the islands
There was an abundance of food:
Crabs, clams, oysters, mussels, sea-urchins, herring,
Seal, flounder, sole, cod, halibut, octopus, and squid.
Large clams were dried and saved on cedar strands
For trade and for the short days of winter.

Each year, just when the earth renewed herself
Once again in the steady warmth of the sun,
By the strength of his memory
The most Noble Salmon would return,
Leading all of his salmon relatives into the wide bays
And up the cool, freshwater rivers.

This was a time for the People to rejoice
And to explain their need for food to the salmon
Who in their desire to continue the life of their own kind
Would fill the rivers from side to side.
The salmon scouts sought the shaded, sandy banks
Of streams high in the distant mountains.

Those among the People acknowledged as fishermen
Would take only the salmon that were needed.
They sang special songs to the salmon, coaxing them
Into entering narrow rock or pole passage ways,
That led to small openings sometimes guarded by sharp,
Pointed stakes, which were one way entrances into baskets
Or pools from which there was no escape.

In shallow waters the men were quick and accurate
With long poles whose barbed and tethered bone points
Would enter deep into the soft flesh of the thrashing fish.

In the bays fishermen would sometimes let out a net
Woven from nettle, hemp, and cedar strands that hung
Like an open purse between their anchored canoes,
Closing it around the salmon when they came
Running with the flow of the tide.

The first warm days were the time for chosen
Women to begin gathering roots and berries
To dry for the long winter gatherings.
Salmon flesh and eggs would also be air-dried
Or smoked over low alder wood fires
And hung from the cedar pole rafters of the long houses.
This was all food the women prepared
For the days when life slept deep in the earth,
And few salmon moved in the icy waters.

When the winds began to cool and the sun traveled
In an arc nearer to the jagged edges of the far, white mountains,
Those chosen to be hunters would stalk elk, deer, and bear,
Moving up silently with bow and spear into the nearby hills.
Sometimes, if the hunting party was large, the hunters
Would encircle and drive the frightened animals
Toward a cliff edge where the animals would panic
And plunge to their death on the rocks below.

All of this work provided good meat, grease, sinew
And hides for clothing and carrying.
There was great respect for the animals
That presented themselves to the hunters
So that the People could live.

The Teachings

*"I feel sorrow for the loss of the old order.
Everything fit together like pieces in a jigsaw
puzzle; all pieces made a beautiful picture.
Everyone was always fed."*

BERTHA DAN [QUAL-SO-LITZA], SWINOMISH

*"Pray that God will give to you good hands,
good eyes, good ears, so that you will truly
be able to feed, to see, to hear. Only then
will you be able to understand
the spiritual ways of the Indian People."*

VELMA CAYOU, SWINOMISH

During the long rains, during the dark days and nights,
When north winds could suddenly clothe earth and trees
With a shawl, white as mountain goat's wool,
The People renewed their courage, and hope,
And sense of caring for one another and for all beings
And powers that made up the whole Circle of Life
Here on this earth.

Ancient stories about the Animal People
Who were on this earth before the human beings came
Told children how and where their People
First appeared, and about mysterious beings
That placed and shaped the rocks, rivers, beaches,
Marshes and mountains that were their People's Home.

In the stories about the Animal Beings
There was everything to be learned about becoming
A human being: the nobility of being honest,
Generous, kind, hard-working, respectful of Elders,
And caring for the young. There was also
Much to be learned about the foolishness of being
Dishonest, stingy, envious, lazy, treacherous,
Caring for no one but oneself.

Large families who lived secure in the longest homes
With easy access to beaches and bays
Where there was an abundance of food
Were families that could share many beautiful gifts
With visiting relatives. Their children and grandchildren,

Who had much time to listen to the good advice of Elders,
Were the luckiest of human beings.

Some of the head men from the wealthiest families
Rose up to great prestige and power.
They were both feared and respected.

Families who lived in crowded houses
With no access to the best beaches
Had few gifts of beauty to share with relatives
At the long winter gatherings. Their children,
Seeking food and warmth, had little time
To listen to the surviving Elders.
These children were the least fortunate of human beings,
Condemned like slaves to a life with no honor and no freedom.

The People's Medicine

"There was a time when medicine people were feared. My great-grandmother was a tiny little woman. She used a walking stick to get around. Yet people were terrified of her."

KENNY MOSES, SR. [KWA-KHWAY-CHUB], SNOQUALMIE

"Sometimes, when we are badly frightened, what we call our su-lee, our soul, just falls off of us. We become confused and sad. It takes someone very special to help us. They must find our soul and put it back on us, or we will never get better."

MARY CAGEY [GWA-TOL-E-MOO], LUMMI

Men and women who could see the unseen,
The inmost center of a person's being,
And the presence of the dead;
Men and women who could feel and recognize
The presence of hidden movements of energy,
Forces that seemed to move from deep within
And around all that could be seen and touched;

These men and women were treated with a respect
That sometimes felt like fear tightening the stomach.
Because these men and women could hear, and feel,
And see the hidden and the mysterious, the movement
Of the sun and the stars, the coming and going of the salmon
And of all the animals, they could tell a person and a People
What they needed to do to stay alive. They could see
When a person's inmost being had left him
And was being pulled toward the place of the dead.
These men and women, helped by a Song,
Could travel to search for and find what was lost
And bring it back to be placed in the sick person.

Some had the right words to ward off harmful thoughts and forces.
Others, working in Song with cedar poles or boards
Alive with power, would cleanse the long, winter homes
Of any clouds of confusion and bitterness
That burdened the People with sadness.
Often while they were working for the People
They would be given Visions that they would share
To help the People understand what they were enduring

And what they had to do to ensure their future together
In harmony with all of the seen and unseen presences
And forces that moved within and around them.

There were also men and women who knew all of the earth's
Roots, barks, leaves, flowers, and berries that could gently
And quickly restore a human being to balance and health.
Only certain ones had this knowledge passed down to them,
A knowledge vast and precise and absolutely necessary
For Peoples seeking the strength and clarity needed
For a long and vibrant life together.

The Most Wonderful Gift

"When the spirit powers came to me, they
were very strong. I could not resist them.
I could not help but sing the Songs.
Now they are always there when I need them.
Whenever there is work to be done. For me
it is like praying. I work to help people."

KENNY MOSES, SR. [KWA-KHWAY-CHUB], SNOQUALMIE

"My mother had a song for traveling.
When my brother went over seas,
she felt that her Song had left her.
She knew it was protecting him.
We were heading back to our old place
on Bow Hill when her Song came back.
She said, 'I know my son is back,'
before anyone told her."

IDA WILLIAMS [HYTWHA], SWINOMISH

The People's most valued gift from the unseen world
Was a movement of strong energy that would rush
From the center of a man or woman's body

Up through throat and lips in a burst of breath
That was a cry becoming a Song.
The force of this song was so great
That tears would flow and the body move
In a dance both free and disciplined,
Just at the edge of a man or woman's
Knowing and control.

Power went out to all of the People gathered,
Power went out from men and women carried
By the breath of their People singing with the sound
And force of wind racing down from the mountains.
This energy moved dancers in a wide circle
Around the Long House fires taking them
Back to the safety of helpers and family who waited
Where the Song had begun.

These Songs were most often brought out
During the long night gatherings
When the sun seemed to travel far away.
Many relatives would gather in the larger cedar homes

For food, and good advice, and stories and dances
About the first beings that prepared the Earth
For the arrival of human beings.

Sometimes there might be a formal memorial
For beloved ones who had died years before.
The beloved's Song would be remembered and sung again;
Their dancing gear would be shown to the Peoples gathered
With the utmost respect.

Sometimes there might be formal Names given
With due regard for those Elders who held in their vast
And accurate memories the generations of Names, and the rights
Associated with those Names according to the gifts
And privileges owned by each of the family lines.

At these winter gatherings along with an abundance of food
Many gifts were shared: capes, blankets, hard wood spoons,
Cedar bowls and boxes.
But the greatest gifts shared were the Songs
That carried the People through the dark nights.

Like rain water held for a moment in the high branches
Of the tall cedars, then released to shower gently
Upon the dark earth below,
These Songs came down, moistening hearts,
Renewing the inmost roots of the People's being.

These Songs came down, visiting the villages
Sending strength out like medicine
To the life sleeping within all things,
Until the sun returned, and light would fill
Mountain and valley, marsh, river, and sea,
With the green motion of life.

Part Two

The Long and Hard Journey

AFTER THE NEW BEINGS CAME

"There was much death, measles and pneumonia. Often there was no food. Many children were orphans."

LAURA EDWARDS [TA-LEQ-TALE], LUMMI-LOWER SKAGIT

When the new beings came,
Something rode with them inside their tall canoes,
Something more dangerous to the People
Than the screams and sudden raids by painted
Warriors from islands far to the north.
Death rode with the new beings.
Death.

Soon whole villages took sick.
Healers could not stop sicknesses
That they had never seen. In the long, cedar homes
Family watched family seized by sweats and fevers.
They saw the bodies of dear ones covered with blisters
And sores. They witnessed nights of moaning and weeping.

And then there was only silence.
Endless silence.

Villages became tombs.
There was no one alive to bury the dead.
From generations of Peoples who lived and moved
Through the islands and up the rivers in multitudes
As numerous and free as the upriver rush of salmon
Each spring, from Peoples whose greetings and Songs
Filled the air of valleys with sounds as various
As the calls of hundreds of ducks and geese,
Whose voices rose and sank over the marshes
Like new snow, blown and falling,

Only a few survived.

THE SURVIVORS

"Our ancestors said that strangers would be coming with white skin and hair on their faces. They would be called 'Changers' because they would change everything. Nothing would ever be the same."

VI HILBERT [TAQW-SHA-BLU], UPPER SKAGIT

"Our loved ones are not gone. They glow on the other side. We have more relatives on the other side than we do on this side."

BERTHA DAN [QUAL-SO-LITZA], SWINOMISH

Grass and vines tried to cover the sites
Of the ancient villages, where trees still held
The bones of the ancient ones. These old ones' minds
Once graced land and water with memories
That reached back to the work of the first animal beings
Who had prepared and shaped everything
For the coming of humankind.

The Survivors,
Some now sharing children with the new beings,
Had to consider a new way of living
On the earth and waters.

Short, square houses with dull eyes
Now leaned toward one another on banks of mud
Near bays where trees drowned in the soiled water.
The new beings grew more numerous.

Each day more arrived from the south and east
Struggling in groups over the high mountain passes.
Some mornings there was the wonder of an horizon
Filled with sails shining, and soon the beaches
Would be shaking with an energy, awkward, restless,
As if it were uncomfortable with itself.

To the remaining People
It seemed as if their world was vanishing.
They were told to leave the places
That had been their joy forever.

They returned home after summer fishing
To find their Long Houses burned to the ground.

Those who were not even close relatives
Were told to live together in areas
Away from where the outsiders were living.
The People felt they were losing
Everything they had ever known.

Tall Hats and Marks on Papers

"We signed the papers with our thumbs.
As soon as the ink was dried, the surrounding
peoples challenged our treaties
and the fight began.
They told us to be self-sufficient after secluding us
on a rock pile. All of the best land
was given to the white farmers."

Robert Joe, Sr. [Wa-wal-ton], Swinomish

"How many meetings do we need to have to tell you
that we are the First Nations Peoples? You tend
to compare us too much with foreign countries
unlike us. We stand on our customs. We were
happy Peoples until the Europeans came with
all of their laws to control us."

Edward Thomas [Kiet-Kanum], Cowichan

Outsiders appeared who said that they were sent
From the east, from far beyond the distant mountains.
They wore tall, black hats and held papers in their hands
Stiff as their manner of standing and sitting.

There were marks all over these papers
Which these newcomers considered very important.

It was the practice of these strangers,
Often with hair all over their faces,
To try and gather some of the head men
From the few remaining villages that waited
Along the sloping edges of the bays and rivers.

They would ask these men to make another mark
On the papers, promising their Peoples
Their own places to fish, hunt, and gather.
These men were told through interpreters
That these places and rights would be protected
And would belong to their Peoples forever.

They were told that help would be given
To fight the new sicknesses among the Peoples.
It was explained to them that there would be teachers
For their children to help them understand the newcomers'

Powers and ways of doing things. There was also mention
Of learning to grow food in the moist earth.

There was no choice but to sign the papers.
They were the color of the sky after rain.
Every day more newcomers came, moving their families
Into the most beautiful bays and valleys.

Even up in the high mountains men were climbing
And cutting into cedars that had stood forever.

Two men would pull a long piece of steel between them
Until beauty in giant form fell, shaking the earth,
Leaving an empty circle in the gray sky,
And an absence of presence and wind-song as shocking
As the silence of villages abandoned to Death.

Some of the head men gathered their remaining strength
To push the newcomers back.
There was even talk of joining with relatives
From over the mountains in an effort to drive

The strangers away.
But there were too many outsiders,
And too many soldiers with guns
That could kill many men at the same time.

Some of the People's warriors were hunted down
And taken to thick walled buildings
With no openings to see in or out.
Their strong arms and legs were bound with chains.
They were led up onto high platforms where they stood
Before the hard eyes of the newcomers' families,
Until the wood fell from beneath their feet,
And their last Songs disappeared into the smoky air,
And with the Songs any hopes that their People had
Of remaining free.

Some
New Visions

"Our Elders had a direct line to God.
When they spoke in their own language,
they brought out what God wanted them
to bring out. They couldn't read or speak
in English, but they knew and spoke of all
the things that are found in the Bible."

Norma Johnston, Swinomish-Samish

"My parents believed in Church
with their whole hearts."

Rita Johnnie [Shwul-latz-tonat], Cowichan

From the newcomers who had come to trade with them,
Some of them with dark eyes and brown skin like their own,
The People had learned through hand signs and trade language
About beings that lived in the unseen world
And words and songs that called in their presence and power.

These beings were said to be beyond the horizon of Light
That fills the sky and holds the earth and waters every dawn.

The Elders respected the energy with which some
Of the newcomers spoke about their visions
Of the unseen world.

Now there were visitors coming among the People
Who seemed to believe even more strongly in these visions.
Some wore wide, wool clothing and had wives
Who helped them in their teaching.
Some were men who seemed to have no wife
Or family. These men, dressed in black robes,
Spoke in many languages and seemed at home with the People.
They taught by using sticks with many marks on them
And pictures on paper, joined together by many dots and lines.

There were stories that went with the marks and pictures
And some of the remaining Elders learned them well.
The leaders among the People were hungry to know anything
That might help them understand why these newcomers
Had arrived, why so many of their dear ones had died,
Why their world was being changed again and again
At a pace that they could not comprehend or accept.

The Elders looked for new energies,
New help coming from the Unseen
That would help their People to survive.
Some among the People found joy and peace when
These messengers spoke about the same things
In the unseen part of the world, a being
Who loved them like a father, and his son,
Jesus, shedding his blood to protect them,
And a great, new energy called holy spirit,
Wide and powerful as the sky that held everything.

The People sang new songs and said prayers
In their own village tongues and in the trade language.
They hoped these songs and prayers
Would bring greater luck to their families.
They felt that they understood Jesus' heart,
Respecting him because he saw their suffering.

The messengers of these new understandings,
Those in the wool suits and skirts, and those in the black robes,
Seemed to not like one another. They spoke badly

Of one another, calling each other liars.
They seemed to want to fight over the People's attention.

These newcomers' dreams and visions showed them a way
Of building very tall houses. In some of these houses
There were a table and bells, and many candles, statues and pictures.
In other tall houses there was a thick book, open upon a stand.
The People were told that they had to choose which house to visit.
They couldn't go and be friendly in all of the tall houses.

SEEKING THE GOOD PLACE

"The missionaries came to my People with a lot of do's and don'ts; among them was the command not to eat meat on Fridays. One day a priest paid a surprise visit on an Elder whom he had baptized with the name, Peter. Well, it happened to be on Friday, and Peter was cooking deer meat in a kettle over the fire. 'Aha,' said the priest, 'You are going to eat meat on Friday!' Peter thought for a minute and then answered the priest: 'When you baptize me you ask me to give up my Indian name and become Peter. Well, before I put deer in the pot I place water on his head and I name him fish!'"

ROBERT JOE, SR. [WA-WAL-TON], SWINOMISH

"When I was a small child I sat on my dad's shoulders for the walk to mass at Lummi. The People loved the priest for his kindness in teaching about our God."

LAURA EDWARDS [TA-LEQ-TALE], SWINOMISH-LOWER SKAGIT

These messengers spoke of a place
Where the dead lived and were happy.
They said that the People would go there, too,
If they washed in the water and followed the new way.

They also talked often about a bad place
Where those went who weren't washed
And who didn't follow the new way.
They said that there were beings that came out
From this dark place in the unseen world
Who would try to confuse and hurt the People,
And take them to this bad place.

The men in the black robes also told the People
That they had a kind mother in the unseen world
And other helpers, ancestors, and friends,
Who really cared about the health and good luck
Of all their families.

The messengers with the new words of power
And the new song seemed to care about the warmth

And health and learning of the People.
But it seemed like they wanted the People
To forget all of their own Songs and stories.
These Songs and stories had forever opened up
The People's understanding of the powers
Within the unseen part of the world.

These Songs and stories helped the People get along
With one another and with all beings that shared life
On the earth and in the waters.
The messengers got angry and scolded the People
Whenever they found out about a night gathering
For the old ceremonies.

The messengers seemed to distrust the healing work
Done by some of the Elders. They seemed afraid
And confused by the strength of the Songs.
They also saw worries in the People's eyes,
Concerns hidden from them
That the People would not talk about.

They began to say that the healers were dealing with bad beings
From the darkest parts of the unseen world.

The Elders knew that powers from the unseen part of the world
Could be used to harm as well as heal.
They would try to know the hearts, the intentions
Of those doing this work. They would try to know
The hearts of those asking for work to be done.

But to consider all of the ceremonies,
All the ways of singing and seeing
And interpreting the unseen presences and powers,
And the wishes of the Beloved shown in dreams,
As bad, as something to be abandoned, forgotten,
This was very hard to accept.

To be asked to wear different clothes and speak new greetings
Was only a little awkward.
To be asked to give up a way of seeing the world,
A way old and sacred beyond memory,
This was unimaginable.

It was like having enemies trying to take away
Their inmost beings, leaving only their bodies,
Thrown and forgotten like empty shells upon the beach.

These demands left the People stunned;
It was as if their breath was leaving them.
The old ones' eyes began to be glazed over
With infinite layers of sadness,
And the light that once danced upon their faces
Sank far within.

THE NEW TEACHERS

"They took me to boarding school when I was only five. I could speak my language and knit socks. I used to pull wool off of the school blankets to knit with. They whipped me for this. I lost my language. They will never be able to take away our Indian religion, our self respect, our respect for others' feelings."

LIZ CASSIMERE [THI-AT-LI-AH], TSAWOUT

"The new teachings were harsh, forcing us to do things we didn't understand. If we didn't do things right, we were going to hell. There was always something wrong."

NORMAN UNDERWOOD [TSIE-QA-LEM], TSAWOUT

Soon some men and women called teachers were telling
Parents and grandparents that their children should leave them
And go away to live in the big houses they called schools
Where they could learn the newcomers' ways
Of measuring, figuring, and talking.

The new teachers might just as well have taken
The grandparents' hearts right out of their bodies.
Yet the grandparents hoped that the new teachers
Would help their children and grandchildren to survive
In a world that they no longer recognized or understood.
It was a world that the old ones could no longer live in.

They became silent, not wanting to tell their children
About the blanket of loneliness, soaked with tears
For their Beloved,
That fell heavy over their shoulders
And pushed their bones into the ground.

Grandfathers and grandmothers knelt at night by the table
Running through their fingers circles of worn beads.
These beads held the faces of their children
Strung together by a single thread of love
And lifted up to the face of Jesus, and to the face of Mary,
Sadness recognizing sadness,
Sadness with tears like the rain falling.

Large boats pushing black smoke out of their insides
Came to take the children away to schools.
Sometimes parents and grandparents brought their children
In family canoes in journeys lasting two or three camps
Just so that they could spend a few more days
With these little ones whom they loved as life itself.
The grandparents secretly hoped that the young ones
Would learn skills and powers from these new "Changers"
Whose knowledge and ways were changing
The whole visible world.

At the schools children were punished
For speaking their own languages. They were forced
To move their mouths and minds into shapes and sounds
And thoughts that they had never considered before.
It seemed that the new teachers wanted the children
To walk and dress like the ones they called soldiers,
Men who enjoyed walking stiffly back and forth
In front of their tall, white houses.

Little ones sometimes did not see their grandparents again;
These grandparents who knew the stories
Of how their People came to be;
These grandparents whose warm understanding and love
Gave meaning to all forms of life on this good earth.

The new teachers did not see any good in the old ways.
They wanted the People to become like them,
Wearing the same clothes, speaking the same language,
Seeking the same jobs, acting toward one another, to the earth,
And to all living things the same way that they did.

They seemed not to see the fear and the sadness
In the eyes of both the old and the young.
They seemed to have no idea of how much
They were ordering the People to give up,
A whole way of understanding themselves within all
Of the seen and unseen world.

They seemed not to care that they were forcing
A People to exist no longer as a People,

Special in the eyes of all living beings.
They did not seem to realize that they were asking the People
To take out their hearts
And leave them in the old trees near the ancient villages
Where their ancestors walked at night
And waited.

At Home No Longer

"I married a Samish man.
Alfred was my husband.
Samish People were asked to leave the island
where all the People lived. The island was
bought up by different ones. I prayed
and prayed for my husband.
The Samish were not being recognized by the government.
Why? The People still lived there. They had
an oyster business there."

LAURA EDWARDS [TA-LEQ-TALE], LUMMI-LOWER SKAGIT

"The white men gave the Indians cows. They scared
you when they ran wild through the woods. Some
of the People would go away to gatherings,
forgetting that cows needed to be milked every day.
The white men cut down all the great trees
And ran a railroad right through the land.
Everyone was poor. Everyone helped everyone.
I was midwife for my friend. And she was
midwife for me. We didn't give money to each other."

MARYA MOSES, SNOHOMISH

"We have Indian Law in our Long House.
We need to keep this law in our hearts."
MAXINE WILLIAMS [TSEN-TSUN-QUA-MAU], SWINOMISH

The People were told to divide the last land
That they stood upon into small pieces.
The government surveyors drove steel markers
Into the soft earth, separating family from family.
These families were used to sharing the land
In humble homes on the beaches and waters.

The men and women hunted and fished, and worked
Small farms and orchards. Men got silver dollars for logging
Allotments. Most families had enough to get by,
Traveling once a month to buy or trade for wool pants
And cotton dresses, for flour, beans, sugar, coffee, kerosene
At the little stores that appeared here and there
In the long river valleys. There was usually enough to share
So that everyone could carry on.

Soon, more outsiders were among the People,
Claiming the remaining land as their own.
The outsiders kept coming. They wanted the best
Bays and beaches, and the thick timber land.
Pushed to the side of the muddy roads that reached
Like long fingers far back into the darkness
Of the remaining trees, the People began to struggle
To find their way to one another.
Sometimes a stack of dollars offered for some family land
Meant the surety of a few months food, or a warmer house,
Or sometimes enough whisky to dull the feeling
Of losing everything.

Small groups of stores called towns began to grow
Near to where the People lived. Some of the newcomers
Were friendly and generous. Some married in.
Others stared at the People in a way that made them feel
Afraid and cold, unwanted, lifeless.
It began to seem that there was no longer a place for them
On the earth and waters where their ancestors had lived

Forever.
Sadness fell across the People's chests
Like heavy stones crushing their ribs.
Sadness turned to loneliness,
Tuberculosis taking lives, taking years
Of lives in faceless hospitals with long, bare corridors
As dark as the night that now fell
Over the People's hearts.
Influenza also descended on the People,
Severe and unexpected, like the coldest winter storm.
Parents and grandparents lost their children.
Children lost their parents and grandparents.

The Federal Government began telling the Elders
That their ways of seeking and making choices
For the People were no longer acceptable.
The People would have to elect councils and deal
With surrounding governments in the borrowed language.
This confused many of the Elders.

This was not their way of gathering and listening
To voices so that the more true might appear
And the People find a way forward together.
There seemed to be no place to acknowledge
Messengers and messages from the unseen part of the world,
No place for the depth of dreams to be pondered, weighed,
And followed.

The Cost of Wars

*"I wish we could have had an alcohol recovery
program for our veterans after World War II.
I think most of our veterans died
after they came home."*

Bernie Gobin [Kia-Kia], Snohomish

*"My son was prayed for by his grandparents
before he went to war. They put hands on him
and sang for him, so that the bullets
would not hurt him."*

Marya Moses, Snohomish

*"We were about to cross this rice field at night.
Suddenly this grizzly bear and this wolf appeared
in front of me. I froze in my tracks. I could see
the hair on the wolf's neck standing up. I told the
company commander that we should not go further
ahead. He listened to me. We circled around behind
the rice field and discovered the enemy waiting to
ambush us. We surprised them*

and were able to kill them all.
The wolf was a guardian in my grandmother's family.
The grizzly bear was what my grandfather had.
He was up in the mountains and saw this beautiful
young girl walking towards him across the meadow.
Suddenly that girl turned into a grizzly bear.
He wanted to run. But he knew right then
that was his power."

RAYMOND MOSES [TI-AT-MUS], SNOHOMISH

Soon many of the men were going away to become soldiers,
Eager to test their courage in battle,
Wanting to fight for the land that they knew
Had always been their People's home.

The women worked endless hours in the canneries,
Their hands numb, their feet swollen from the cold.
Some women worked in shipyards and factories
In the big cities that appeared at night
Like lonely monsters with a thousand eyes
Wrapped around the waters of the once quiet bays.

After the war the men who came home fished
And fought with steel against the trees,
And with whiskey against their own bodies.
They were weighted with memories they could tell
To no one.

In the spring and summer families from all reservations
Traveled on flatbed trucks to the warmer valleys,
Helping farmers with the harvest.
Bone games lasted all night
And boys and girls finally discovered
Boys and girls beyond the world of cousins.

On the long weekends arms that pulled racing canoes
Hurled and hit baseballs with accuracy and power.
Brothers to the north trained their legs and lungs for soccer.
The women watched,
Carrying inside of them the future of their People,
Clinging to a belief in the goodness of life itself,
Knowing in a quiet way that their children and grandchildren
Needed love as much as their husbands needed honor.

Soon the men were called to fight again
Far away against an enemy without number
On bare Korean hills that arched over their bodies
Like enormous tombs in the gray depth of winter.
At home the women carried on,
Making the hard choices that would carry and clothe
And feed their children for another week,
Another month of days.

The eyes of the men who came home
Were much older than the strong, fresh eyes
Of the young men in stiff, new uniforms
That looked out from most living room walls.
The men's faces and bodies seemed to be haunted
By a terrible and crushing secret
That they often drank to forget.

"RELOCATION" OR DISLOCATION

"What we are still trying to do is to tell the American public who we were and what we are now."

CHESTER CAYOU, SR. [TI-SE-LUCHT], SWINOMISH

"We were taught to never give up. We traveled all over the country fighting on behalf of Indian tribes. We will never be done in this work."

ROBERT JOE, SR. [WA-WAL-TON], SWINOMISH

Federal Government leaders got the old idea
That it would be good to "terminate" reservations.
Government officials began telling the People
That it was best for them to leave their communities
And "relocate" for a sure job in the bigger cities.

Some were able to leave family and relatives
And the feeling of being near their own People.
But for many "relocation" became isolation
And the last dollars for on-the-job training
Bought enough gas and parts for the long journey

Home to stand on the last piece of land
Where their hearts would let them say
That they belonged.

Strong tribal speakers with a vision
Of their People's past and future
Took up the fight against the power of a handful
Of dollars offered in exchange for centuries of treaty rights.
They sought out allies in the congress and senate
And finally turned back the tide of contempt
That they knew would have swept their People
Into oblivion.

Viet Nam

The young men went there seeking honor.
Pictures of their fathers and grandfathers had looked
At them since they were little, young men smiling
In their starched uniforms, arms draped over the shoulders
Of buddies who never returned home.

Viet Nam. A place of extraordinary beauty
Turned into a swamp of confusion and pain.
Men who would have been heroes at another time
Came home soiled, dishonored by political forces fouled
Beyond anyone's comprehension.

Forgotten, abandoned by the country
That had asked for the gift of their lives,
They reinforced their restlessness
With the use of marijuana, alcohol, heroin,
Cocaine, and speed. Their disappointment
Took them into a sad solitude that their wives and children
Could not understand or enter.

Grandparents kept the children
While the young women went to college,
Becoming nurses and social workers, teachers and lawyers.
These women wanted their dedication and energy
To carry their People beyond the wreckage of despair.
They were looking for the hearts of their husbands to join them,
But they could not find them.

THE
RETURN
OF THE
SONGS

*"God himself is our culture. He comes to us
in visions of love and brotherhood. We believe
in the words of our Elders and try to live them.
Our Songs are to bring peace to the People."*
ROBERT GEORGE [SITZ-WAH-NOOCH], TSLEIL-WAUTUTH

*"There will be a call, a ringing in your ears,
a clear thought, a Song, to love God,
and to encourage others."*
LANDY JAMES, SWINOMISH

The great-grandmothers and great-grandfathers
Sought life for their People.
They wanted to share what they had in their pockets,
To pass on the advice that their grandparents
Had entrusted to them. They wanted
To steer the steps of their children and grandchildren
Onto a good and lasting path.

But these children had for a long time
Heard different songs than the ones

The grandparents sang in the early morning
Or before they rested at night.

The young listened to songs with no meaning,
Songs that could not last or carry anyone,
Loud and strident songs that drowned out
Their great-grandparents' gentle voices.

The great-grandparents had to open their hands
And let their children follow strange voices
That would lead only to Death,
Which ate up their children with a more angry
Appetite than any monster in the ancient stories.

Then, after many years, something different
Started to happen. The young sought to hear Songs
That they had never heard before.
Their parents began to hear Songs similar in sound
To the Songs that they once had heard
Their grandparents singing. The old timers
Began to be looked for and to be heard again.

The People began to feel their own presence
And their own voice.
They knew from deep within themselves
That they were not a vanquished or a vanished race.
They were wounded. Yes.
They were survivors of a holocaust. Yes.
But they were alive and here to stay.

A Time for Deciding

"This Long House was our parliament. Our laws were passed down here. Here Seeyowin takes place. Our Elders' tears remain on the ground, making it sacred, helping us to know who we are."

NORMAN UNDERWOOD [TSIE-QA-LEM], TSAWOUT

"My families were hunters and fishers. I went to school to learn to fight for thirty years over paper protecting my people's rights. Why couldn't I just have been home providing food for my village? Generation after generation suffers under the impact of colonialism. Where does it stop? How does it stop?"

DAVID PAUL [SAPELEQ], TSARTLIP

Speakers stepped forward to say
That their People's hearts were so joined
To ancient lifeways on land, sea, and water
That no one, no government, no organization, no state
Or Province could ever take this from them.

Men and women from among the People
Were beaten and thrown into jails.
They were feared and laughed at
By some of their own.
But the evil powers that chained
And hanged some of their ancestors,
The lying tongues that broke
Their great-grandparents' hearts,
Could not silence the new voices.

There were egos involved;
There were mistakes made.
The new leaders were sometimes
As confused and wounded as those
Who tried to follow them.
But the voice of the People
Could not be silenced.

Both the young and the old timers
Were once again seeking the Songs,

Their People's oldest medicine
To sustain and guide them.
Nothing could stop this.

Nothing can stop it now,
Unless the People forget who they are,
Forget the land that they stand on,
Forget the waters that they fish,
Forget the words and Songs entrusted to them,
Forget their own children.

Nothing can silence this Voice now,
Except weakness from within;
The People listening to other words and songs
That carry with them only Death,
And the putrid smell of greed and selfishness
That rises like a nighttime fog
Hiding the rotting bones of a civilization

That in its mad desire to conquer and control
Everything, lost its own meaning,
Its own hope,
And its own soul.

Part Three
The Holy

SEEKING UNDERSTANDING, SEEKING WISDOM

*"This Long House was
and is our first Church.
We treat it as something sacred.
My father taught that Long House
and Catholic teachings run parallel."*

NORMAN UNDERWOOD [TSIE-QA-LEM], TSAWOUT

*"We come into the Long House to change our
way of life, to give ourselves to the Spirit.
If you believe down deep, your Song will come
to you. The Song will sing you. Our work
in the Long House brings the best out of us."*

ROBERT JOE, SR. [WA-WAL-TON], SWINOMISH

*"The spirits will recognize anything that we do
the best we can. Sometimes we are not sure
exactly how to do things right. But when we do
the best we can, it is accepted."*

BERTHA DAN [QUAL-SO-LITZA], SWINOMISH

What paths are open to the People?
Who is there to look toward and listen to?

Is it not still good to look toward the most respected
Grandmothers and grandfathers who still follow
The Seeyowin and Christian ways of living,
The path of understanding and kindness,
The path of love and forgiveness?

The great-grandparents show to us
Minds open to the good in all things,
And hearts that can endure all of the pain
That there is in our world.

They hold onto a Vision showing
That the goodness in all living beings
Cannot be crushed by suffering and death,
Only reborn in a new manner
Beyond anything that we ever hoped for.

The old-timers know that deep down
Inside all things there lives an awareness,
An energy, a movement of power and beauty
That we name life.

They know that there is always a lesson
To be learned, a suffering to be endured,
A Song to be heard and cherished.

They know that no thing and no one is
Totally defeated, that Something goes on,
Something that runs like blood in the veins of the People,
Something that remembers and carries all,
Something that holds the roots of all plants and trees,
Something that breaks into shapes and bursts
Into colors as bright as lightning,
Something that shakes the earth with thunder,
Something wide as the most distant waters,
Something bold as the eyes of the winged hunters
And old as the grandfather heron who watches everything.

This energy, this movement is lasting
And seems without limit.
The grandmothers know this.
They have carried this energy within them
And kneaded and shaped its form,

Working it like bread dough in their hands.
They have woven its fiber into loving hearts
Deep and strong enough to hold
The whole world.

The grandfathers know this.
They have felt this power rise like a cry
And carry them in cedar canoes, quick
And light like gulls skimming the water.
They have felt this energy like a fire
Within their bodies, making life.
They have seen this energy flash
Along their nets, playing with their hopes
Like seals stealing salmon.

They have seen it in the bull elk's eyes
Before they took him down from the high mountains
To feed the People.
They, too, know that this energy
Cannot be defeated,
Can only be dreamed and danced again.

MOVING
THROUGH
SADNESS

"My children, pray, pray, pray.
That is all we have in times of trouble.
Why do some families have so many tragic
things happen? We do not know. I only know
that we must pray. It is the only thing that
will carry us through. Look at me! I am
ninety-six years old. If I had not prayed
since I was young, I would not be standing
here before you."

LAURA EDWARDS [TA-LEQ-TALE], LUMMI-LOWER SKAGIT

"Sometimes it takes tragedy to pull us together.
It is up to our speakers to turn our thoughts
back to life. Our Elders used to be able to
draw a picture of what sorrow was. They told
us how it could defeat us. They were uneducated
people but most eloquent in the native tongue. Their
words were like medicine for each one present."

BERTHA DAN [QUAL-SO-LITZA], SWINOMISH

"Healing is as much a part of life as hurting.
It isn't our fault what happened to us
historically. It is our responsibility now
to help ourselves get well."

FAYE BATES [LA-SY-EL], SWINOMISH

There is an immense Sadness.
Sometimes it visits us unexpectedly
Haunting the sides of our awareness,
A darkness rising beneath and behind the house
Of our mind, filling our being
With an anger too large to name.
Can we pretend that this Sadness
Is not there? Can we package and store it
In a forgotten room of our memory?

So much has been lost!
Everything has been altered, changed.
We have come to know again
What the ancient ones knew from the beginning:

The lives of fish and fishermen
Are tightly bound together.

Because forests have been destroyed
High in the mountains,
Because fertilizers and chemicals
Poison the rivers,
Because generations of fishermen
Have left a legacy of waste and greed,
Because dams and their gift, electricity,
Are considered greater goods than the perfect
Beauty of streams and rivers seeking the sea,
The salmon no longer return.

In place of a spirit of generosity and cooperation
There is war out on the water,
Indians against cowboys, tribes against tribes,
Tribes against the state, nation against nation,
All seeking to take the last salmon.

Today the People no longer live around all
Of the wide bays and rivers.
Roads wriggle through the mountains,
Running through the quiet places
Where the old-timers used to bathe and fast
And seek Helpers to guide and protect them.

Songs that used to be heard everywhere
Announcing the goodness and mystery of things
Are mostly forgotten. Languages that still bring
Joy to the great-grandmothers are no longer understood
By their children and grandchildren.

These great-grandmothers were once the little girls
That we now see in the old photos. Their frightened eyes
Show the pain of hearts trapped in cold buildings
And stiff military uniforms.
These great-grandmothers lived when they were young
With a sense of being separated from the unseen powers
That they knew once blessed their Peoples with abundance
And shared with them one single home.

These great-grandmothers knew well the cold gaze
And meaningless words of the countless neighbors
Moving in around them. They knew well
The feeling that they were no longer a People
With a living story, and a common journey.
Their origin and presence on this earth
Was no longer seen and held as sacred.
Their People had somehow become a problem,
A problem to be solved, a problem to be endured,
A problem to be ended, a problem to be forgotten.

And yet, these great-grandmothers, and some grandfathers
Are still here!
Their children and grandchildren are here!
War and disease could not kill them.
A thousand plans could not make them
Like everyone else.
Living beings, not extinct casualties
Of a cruel westward expansion,
Demand back the bones of their ancestors
From universities and museums.

THIS WAY OF GOODNESS

"We watch the salmon in their endless drive to reproduce their own. They survive even with all that has been done to end their abundant life. We need to shape our souls for the sake of our children and grandchildren, so that a life of beauty and dignity will be passed on to them."

PETER WILLIAMS [HUL-QUINUM], COWICHAN

"Your Song will take care of you, your family, your People. Be proud of it. Take care of it."

TIM EDWARDS [STAB-AL-QUID], SWINOMISH

"The eyes of the old-timers looking down are filled with tears of thanks when they see the children talking the language, carrying on in a good way. They nod their heads and say, 'Yes.'"

RAYMOND MOSES [TI-AT-MUS], SNOHOMISH

On the sea and on the rivers,
In the mountains and in the cities,
In courtrooms, classrooms, and legislative halls,

A living People stands and fights for its place on this earth,
For its unique identity and sovereign dignity.

Both old and young seek out and follow
The ancient ways of understanding and generosity
That shaped and guided their great-great-grandparents.
Long Houses are filled with dancers
And Songs warm up the Churches.
Carvers, painters, speakers, teachers, writers
Find forms, colors, and words to embody
New Visions coming to a living People.

Alcohol and drugs, used for generations
To numb the pain of unbearable memories,
Are now unmasked to reveal what they hide:
A flight towards death.

New enemies of the People's well being
Are faced with honesty, courage,
Compassion, and a strategy of resistance.
There is no time for self-pity and self-indulgence.
There is no time for giving up and making excuses.
And yet, Sadness still stalks the People

Like a thief in the depth of night,
Trying all the windows of the village homes,
Moving along the city streets, devouring the forgotten.
Will the People finally disappear?
Will the teachings be lost?

No.
No! Not as long as there is one young man
And one young woman who before their People
Join together with a pledge to each other
And to their children to hold
In the center of their hearts
The way of respect, generosity and kindness
That their ancestors knew and lived.

If there is one young man and one young woman
Hidden within the ordinary life of village or city,
Who before the hard eyes of those who live in worlds
That will never understand them,
Truly care for all children,
This way of Goodness will continue.

If there is one young man and one young woman
Who before the whole world
Follow their great-great-grandparents' way
Of nurturing the fragile voice and movement of life
Within all persons and things,
Then all will not be lost.
Their People will live on.

Their People will live on!

THE PORTRAITS

The Team

Cover: Harold Joseph, Jr., Duwamish-Swinomish, is a grandfather, artist, and educator living on the Tulalip Reservation.

Design: Ann Amberg is an artist and long time advocate for Native American concerns in the Puget Sound area. She is a book/publications designer. She lives in Carnation, Washington.

Photography: Mary Grace Long is an artist/photographer based in Seattle, Washington.

Text: Patrick Twohy is a Jesuit priest who for the past twenty-seven years has lived and worked with Salishan Peoples first on the Northwest Plateau and now in the Puget Sound area. He has written one other book, "Finding A Way Home: Indian and Catholic Spiritual Paths of the Plateau Tribes."

ACKNOWLEDGEMENTS

My hands go up in thanks to members of the talking circles at Swinomish and Nanaimo for their careful reading of this manuscript. Their insights, comments, and corrections, and, above all, their trust in the work was most encouraging to me. Thanks also go out to Catherine Lucia and Barbara Jackson for their careful editing, and to Jay Miller, Ph.D., Fr. Craig Boly, S.J., and the late Denise Levertov for reading and improving the text.

My heart is filled with gratitude to Susanna Hayes, Ph.D., Stevens and Tricia Trainer, Fr. Robert Rekofke, S.J., and so many of my Jesuit brothers for their unending love and support. Special thanks go to Charlie O'Hara, Director of Swinomish Planning, and to his assistant August Rozema for getting the idea of a second edition going; to Chuck Robinson of Village Books, Julia Clarke of Clarke and Stone Books, and John and Sharon Connell of the Next Chapter for their constant advice and encouragement; to Darrell Hillaire, Chairman of the Lummi Tribe, Hank Gobin, Cultural Resources Manager for the Tulalip Tribes, and Joan Staples of the Tahoma Indian Center for their unending support and guidance.

Possible Questions for Use
in a Classroom or Group Setting

What feelings arise and remain in me as I read or hear
Beginnings?

What words, scenes or pictures stand out in my mind?

Does this story remind me of other stories that I have
heard, perhaps stories that have been passed down in my
own family?

Having read this story do I feel encouraged to live my life
in a certain manner?

How would I describe to someone else this manner of
living that I have chosen?